Nine Latin American Folk Songs

Arranged for Solo Voice and Piano • For Recitals, Concerts and Contests

ARRANGED BY BRUCE TRINKLEY • ENGLISH TEXTS BY J. JASON CHARNESKY

Table of Contents

D5

Medium High Book (22933) ....ISBN 0-7390-3375-1
Medium High Accompaniment CD (22934) ....ISBN 0-7390-3376-X
Medium High Book & CD (22935) ....ISBN 0-7390-3377-8
Medium Low Book (22936) ....ISBN 0-7390-3378-6
Medium Low Accompaniment CD (22937)................................ISBN 0-7390-3379-4
Medium Low Book & CD (22938)...ISBN 0-7390-3380-8

Cover Art: Yellow Rose
by Linda Carter Holman (b. 1949)
Photo: Scott Moody
From the collection of Jay Althouse and Sally K. Albrecht

About the Artist: Linda Carter Holman spent part of her childhood in Venezuela, and was brought up in Cushing, OK. At age 20 she began teaching herself to paint, and since then has developed her painting style from naive to highly sophisticated. Her subject matter is frequently women in colorful, imaginative costumes. In addition to paintings, she also works in monoprints, lithographs, and ceramics. She resides in California, and her work can be seen on her website, www.carterholman.com.

Alfred

22936

General Pronunciation Guide for Latin American Spanish

The vowels in Spanish have just one sound:

	IPA	English example	Spanish example
a is pronounced *ah*	[ɑ]	*father*	*amada*
e is pronounced *eh*	[ɛ]	*well*, *met*	*de*
i is pronounced *ee*	[i]	*meet*	*si*, *vivir*
o is pronounced *aw*	[ɔ]	*thought*	*rosa*
u is pronounced *oo*	[u]	*boot*	*tu*

Consonants are similar to English, with the following exceptions:

	IPA	English example	Spanish example
c before *e* or *i* is pronounced *s*	[s]	*city*	*doce*
c before *a, o, u, l,* or *r* is pronounced *k*	[k]	*cast*	*canto*
h is silent		*honor*	*haber*
j is an aspirated *h*	[h]	*hot*	*mujer*
ll is pronounced *y*	[j]	*tortilla*	*estrella*
ñ is pronounced *ny*	[ɲ]	*onion*	*niño*
q, always followed by silent *u*, is pronounced *k*	[k]	*plaque*	*quero*
r, when between two vowels or final, is flipped	[ɾ]	*(no equivalent)*	*suspiro*
r, when doubled, initial, or preceded or followed by a consonant, is rolled	[r]	*(no equivalent)*	*tierras*
y is usually pronounced *y*	[j]	*yes*	*Yo*
y at the end of a word is pronounced *ee*	[i]	*meet*	*voy, ay, y*
z is pronounced *s*	[s]	*song*	*paz*

General Pronunciation Guide for Brazilian Portuguese (5. *Nesta rua* is in Portuguese)

Vowels are similar to Spanish with the following exception:

	IPA	English example	Portuguese example
final *o* is pronounced *oo*	[u]	*boot*	*anjo*

Diphthongs: (Each vowel is approximately equal.)

	IPA	English example	Portuguese example
ão is pronounced *ow*	[ɑu]	*now*	*solidão, coração*
ei is pronounced *ay*	[ɛɪ]	*day*	*roubei*
eu is approximately *eh-oo*	[ɛu]	*(no equivalent)*	*meu*
ou is approximately *oh-oo*	[ou]	*toe*	*roubou*

Nasalizations: *a, e, i, o,* and *u* before a final *m* or *n*, or before *m* or *n* and another consonant, are nasalized. (The *m* and the *n* are not pronounced as such.)

	IPA	English example	Portuguese example
am, an, em, and *en*	[ã]	*(no equivalent)*	*tambem, tem, dentro*
um	[œ]	*(no equivalent)*	*um*

Consonants are similar to Spanish with the following exceptions:

	IPA	English example	Portuguese example
ç is pronounced *s*	[s]	*city*	*coração*
ch is pronounced *sh*	[ʃ]	*shout*	*chama*
j is approximately *zh*	[ʒ]	*vision*	*anjo*

For further information, please consult:

A Singer's Manual of Spanish Lyric Diction by Nico Castel. Published by Excalibur, New York 1994. ISBN: 0962722693

The Pronunciation of Brazilian Portuguese by James P. Giangola. Published by LINCOM Europa, Munich 2001. ISBN: 3895864463

Pronunciation Guide for Choral Literature – French, German, Hebrew, Italian, Latin, Spanish by William V. May and Craig Tolin. Published by MENC, Reston, VA 1978. ISBN: 0940796473

1. VUELA, SUSPIRO
(Fly, My Sighs)

English lyrics by
JASON CHARNESKY

Latin American Folk Song
Arranged by **BRUCE TRINKLEY**

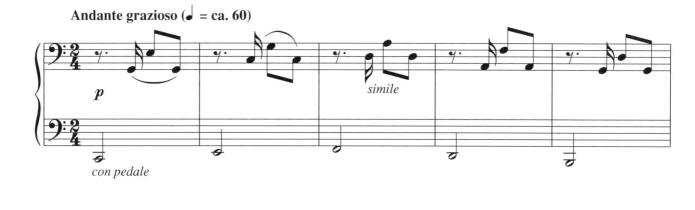

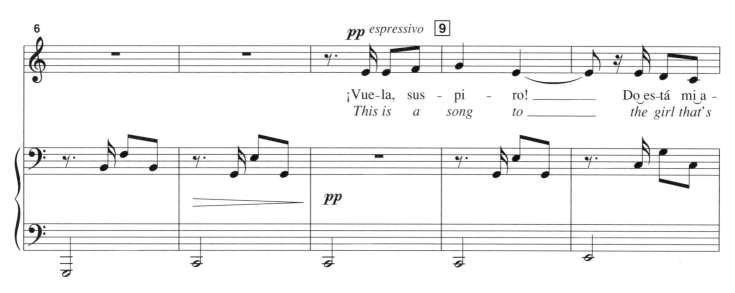

¡Vue-la, sus - pi - ro! _____ Do es-tá mi a -
This is a song to _____ *the girl that's*

ma - da, _____ y de lle - ga - da, _____ sor - prén - de - la. _____
gone, who _____ *has up and wan - dered* _____ *so far a - way.* _____

1. Vuela, suspiro

¡Vuela, suspiro!
Do está mi amada,
y de llegada,
sorpréndela.
Dile que ausente,
penas padezco.
Si se entristece,
consuélala.

1. Fly, My Sighs

Fly, my sighs,
to where my lover lives
and, on arriving,
surprise her.
Say to her that in my absence,
I feel keenly her pain.
If she grieves,
comfort her.

2. ¿DÓNDE VAS, ALFONSO DOCE?
(Where Do You Go, Alfonso XII?)

English lyrics by
JASON CHARNESKY

Latin American Folk Song
Arranged by **BRUCE TRINKLEY**

¿Dón-de vas, Al-fon-so Do-ce? ¿Dón-de vas, tris-te de tí? Voy en bus-ca de Mer-ce-des, que ha-ce tiem-po no la ví. _____ ¿Dón-de

Where do you go, King Al-fon-so, wan-d'ring sad and so for-lorn? I seek out my wife Mer-ce-des, who has van-ished with the morn. _____ Where do

vas, Al - fon - so Do - ce? ¿Dón-de vas, tris - te de tí? Voy en bus - ca de Mer -
you go, King Al - fon - so, pal-lid cheek and tear-ful eye? I seek out my love Mer -

ce - des, que ha-ce tiem - po no la ví.____
ce - des, who was ev - er at my side.____

Tu Mer - ce - des va se ha muer-to; muer-ta es - tá que yo la
Queen Mer - ce - des has de - part-ed. Four dark hors - es grave-ly

vi. Cua - tro Du - ques la lle - va - ban por las ca - lles de Ma - drid. _____
tread, four great dukes car - ry her cof - fin down the dark streets of Ma - drid. _____

holding back

Tempo primo
p [41]

holding back

Tempo primo

Los fa - ro - les de Pa -
Blaz-ing can-dles by the

la - cio ya no quie - ren a - lum - brar, por - que se ha muer - to Mer - ce - des y lu -
hun-dreds used to light her pal-ace yard. Now a sin - gle star at mid-night is the

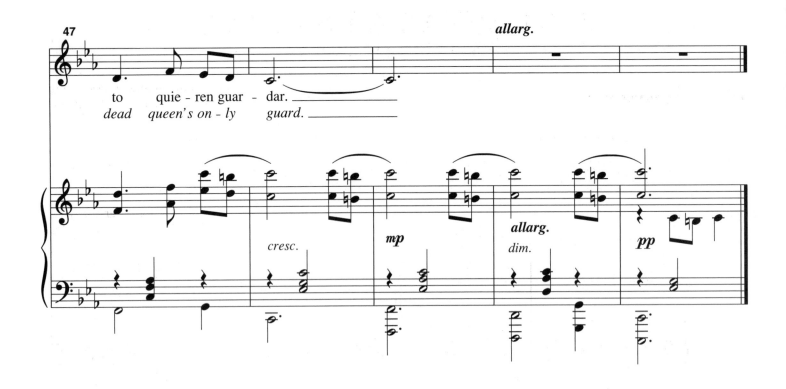

to quie - ren guar - dar. _____
dead queen's on - ly guard. _____

2. ¿Dónde vas, Alfonso Doce?

¿Dónde vas, Alfonso Doce?
¿Dónde vas, triste de tí?
Voy en busca de Mercedes,
que hace tiempo no la ví.

Tu Mercedes va se ha muerto;
muerta está que yo la ví.
Cuatro Duques la llevaban
por las calles de Madrid.

Los faroles de Palacio
ya no quieren alumbrar,
porque se ha muerto
Mercedes y luto quieren guardar.

2. Where Do You Go, Alfonso XII?

Where to now, King Alfonso?
Where to now, o man in pain?
I go in search of Mercedes,
whom I have not seen for a long time.

Your Mercedes has died;
I myself have seen her dead.
Four dukes were bearing her
through the streets of Madrid.

The lanterns of the palace
will no longer be lit,
for Mercedes has died
and they are in mourning.

3. A CANTAR A UNA NIÑA
(When I Sang to a Child)

English lyrics by
JASON CHARNESKY

Latin American Folk Song
Arranged by **BRUCE TRINKLEY**

Lyrics (measures 36–53):

que - lla! Le in - ven - té cien mil nom - bres por ca-da e - stre - lla, por ca-da e -
la - tion! She wish-es there could be twen-ty thou-sand stars need-ing fur-ther

stre - lla. Por fin pa - só la no - che. Lle - gó la au -
stud - y. But all too soon the deep night gives way to

ro - ra. Se fue-ron las e - stre - llas y que - dó so - la.
morn - ing, tak - ing a - way the star - light. Les - sons are o - ver.

Ye - lla de - cí - a, y e - lla de - cí - a: De - bie-ra ha-ber e -
Now I must leave her though it must grieve her. Bright sun! But she and

55 ... *allarg.*

stre - llas tam-bién de dí - a, tam-bién de dí - a.
I gaze in - to the sky to find stars are shin - ing.

allarg.

dim.

3. A cantar a una niña

A cantar a una niña
yo le enseñaba
y un beso a cada nota
siempre le daba.
Y aprendió tanto,
que aprendió muchas cosas
menos el canto.

Conocer las estrellas
también quería.
Yo un beso a cada nombre
le repetía.
¡Qué noche aquella!
Le inventé cien mil nombres
por cada estrella.

Por fin pasó la noche.
Llegó la aurora.
Se fueron las estrellas
ye quedó sola.
Y ella decía:
Debiera haber estrellas
también de día.

3. When I Sang to a Child

When I sang to a child,
I taught her
and gave her a kiss
with every note.
She learned so much,
she learned many things,
except the song.

She also wanted
to know the stars.
For each name
I gave a kiss.
What a night!
I invented a hundred thousand names
for every star.

Finally, the night passed.
The dawn arrived.
The stars were gone
and she remained alone.
And said,
There should be stars
by day as well.

4. MI MAMÁ ME ACONSEJABA
(My Mama Advised Me)

English lyrics by
JASON CHARNESKY

Mexican Folk Song
Arranged by **BRUCE TRINKLEY**

22936

16

22936

18

22936

4. Mi mamá me aconsejaba

Mi mamá me aconsejaba
que no fuera enamorado.
Cuando veo una muchacha
me le voy de medio lado,
Como el gallo a la gallina,
Como la garza a el pescado,
Como la tórtola al trigo,
Como la vieja al cacao.

4. My mama advised me

My mama advised me
not to fall in love.
When I see a young woman
I turn my head:
like the cock to the hen,
like the heron to the fish,
like the turtle dove to the wheat field,
like the old woman to cocoa.

5. NESTA RUA
(On Our Street)

English lyrics by
JASON CHARNESKY

Portuguese Folk Song from Brazil
Arranged by **BRUCE TRINKLEY**

Nes - ta
Down this

ru - a, nes - ta ru - a tem um bos - que _____ Que se
road, oh, down this road there is a for - est, _____ that is

Copyright © MMIV by Alfred Publishing Co., Inc.

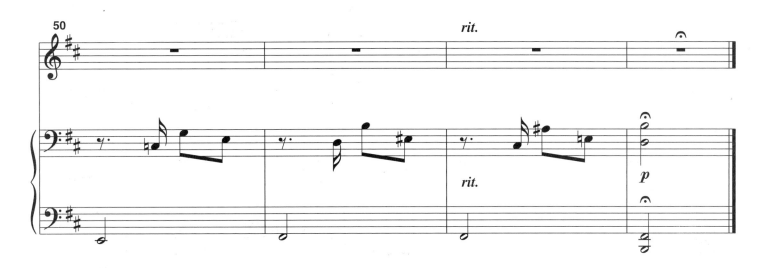

5. Nesta rua (Portuguese)
Nesta rua, nesta rua tem um bosque
Que se chama, que se chama solidão;
Dentro delle, dentro delle mora um anjo.
Que roubou, que roubou meu coração.

Si eu roubei, si eu roubei teu coração,
Tu tambem, tu tambem roubaste o meu;
Si eu roubei, si eu roubei teu coração
É porque, é porque te quero bem.

5. On Our Street
On this road, on this road there is a forest
That is called, that is called solitude.
Inside of it, inside of it there dwells an angel
Who has stolen, who has stolen my heart.

If I've stolen, if I've stolen your heart,
You have also, you have also stolen mine.
If I've stolen, if I've stolen your heart,
It's because, it's because I love you very much.

6. UNA TARDE FRESQUITA DE MAYO
(One Cool Afternoon in May)

English lyrics by
JASON CHARNESKY

Latin American Folk Song
Arranged by **BRUCE TRINKLEY**

ju - ra que nun - ca ha te - ni - do flo - res en la
is the first time you have done this, and I'm en the first

ma - no de o - tra mu - jer. _____ Yo te
girl whose red rose you will wear." _____ Oh, I

ju - ro que e - res la pri - me - ra _____ de quien
swear my sweet dear, I im - plore you, _____ there has

flo - res e - spe - ro te - ner. _____ Por lo
nev - er been an - y be - fore you. _____ May I

6. Una tarde fresquita de Mayo

Una tarde fresquita de Mayo
monté en mi caballo y salí a pasear,
por la senda donde mi morena,
graciosa y hermosa, solía pasar.

Yo la ví que cortaba una rosa.
Yo la ví que cortaba un clavel
y la dije: Jardinera hermosa,
¿me das una rosa? ¿Me das un clavel?

Y ella dijo muy fina y galante:
Al instante yo se los daré
si me jura que nunca ha tenido
flores en la mano de otra mujer.

Yo te juro que eres la primera
de quien flores espero tener.
Por lo tanto, jardinera hermosa,
¿me das una rosa? ¿Me das un clavel?

6. One Cool Afternoon in May

One cool afternoon in May,
I mounted my horse and set out to ride,
to the place where my dark one, graceful
and beautiful, would walk.

I saw her cutting a rose,
I saw her cutting a carnation,
and said to her: "Beautiful gardener,
will you give me a rose, will you give me a
carnation?"

And she said, politely and flirtatiously:
"Immediately, I'll give them,
if you swear that you never have held the
flowers of another woman."

"I swear to you that you are the first from
whom I hope to get flowers.
And so, beautiful gardener,
will you give me a rose, a carnation?"

7. EL CAPOTÍN
(A Little Rain Hat)

English lyrics by
JASON CHARNESKY

Latin American Folk Song
Arranged by **BRUCE TRINKLEY**

22936

se - ré fir - me en el _____ a - mar. Se - ré
I can take what - ev - er may come. Please se -

fir - me en el a - mar _____ y con - stan - te en
lect me. You pro - tect me from the world's hard

el _____ que - rer. ¡Que fa - ti - gas pa - sa un
win - ter - y storm. For a lov - er's like a

hom - bre cuan - do quie - re a u - na _____ mu - jer!
cov - er that can keep one hap - py and warm.

7. El Capotín

No me mates, no me mates,
déjame vivir en paz;
que en estando yo a tu lado
seré firme en el amar.

Seré firme en el amar
y constante en el querer.
¡Que fatigas pasa un hombre
cuando quiere a una mujer!

Con en capotín, tín, tín, tín,
esta noche va a llover,
con en capotín, tín, tín, tín,
a eso del amanecer.

Con en capotín, tín, tín, tín,
esta noche va a nevar,
con en capotín, tín, tín, tín,
a eso de la madrugá.

7. A Little Rain Hat

Do not crush me, do not crush me,
let me live in peace.
For in standing by your side,
I'll be strong in loving you.

I'll be strong in loving you
and constant in my affection.
What anguish a man has
when he loves a woman!

With the little cape,
this night it is going to rain.
With the little cape,
at about dawn.

With the little cape,
tonight it is going to snow.
With the little cape,
at about daybreak.

8. AL PASAR POR SEVILLA*
(On Visiting Sevilla)

English lyrics by
JASON CHARNESKY

Latin American Folk Song
Arranged by **BRUCE TRINKLEY**

*Available for S.A.T.B. voices from Alliance Music Publications in "Dos Canciones de Lorca" (AMP 0363).

lor! _____
no! _____
Me de - spi - do llo - ran - do de _____ mi mo -
You have pleased _ me but I must leave _ you. Fare -

re - na. ¡A - diós, a - diós! _____
well, dear lov - er, good - bye!" _____
Al pa - sar _ por Se -
Stroll-ing down _ old Se -

vi - lla vi a u - na chi - qui - lla y me e - na - mo - ré. _____
vi - lla _ a dark beau - ty _ caught my eye. _____

La to - mé _ de la ma - no y al _ cam - pa -
Hand in hand, we ran off to find _ a field

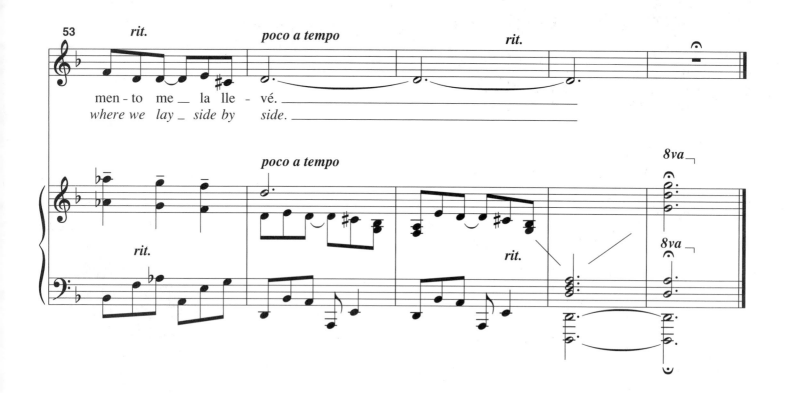

men - to me _ la lle - vé. _____
where we lay _ side by side. _____

8. Al pasar por Sevilla

Al pasar por Sevilla
vi a una chiquilla
y me enamoré.
La tomé de la mano
y al campamento
me la llevé.

Le dije: Sevillana,
rosa temprana,
clavel de olor,
vente conmigo al muelle
y embarcaremos
en un vapor.

El vapor va por agua
y tú por la arena
¡Ay, que dolor!
Me despido llorando
de mi morena.
¡Adiós, adiós!

8. On Visiting Sevilla

On visiting Sevilla,
I saw a young girl
and fell in love.
I took her by the hand
and led her
to the camp.

I said: "Girl of Sevilla,
freshest of roses,
fragrant carnation,
come to the dock
and we'll set off
by ship.

The ship goes by water
and you go by land.
Oh, what sorrow I feel!
My farewell bring sobs
for my dark lass.
Goodbye, goodbye!"

9. VILLANCICO
(Carol)

English lyrics by
JASON CHARNESKY

Puerto Rican Christmas Carol
Arranged by **BRUCE TRINKLEY**

Va-mos, pas-tor-
Let us go, ye

ci - tos, va - mos a Be - lén, que ha na - ci - do el
men, to Beth - le - hem we hur - ry, where the child is

ni - ño; el ni - ño Ma - nuel. ¡El a - gui - nal -
born. To God's own Son we jour - ney. Hear our Christ - mas

22936

9. Villancico

Vamos, pastorcitos,
vamos a Belén,
que ha nacido el niño;
el niño Manuel.

¡El aguinaldillo,
Señora, por Dios!
Que venimos cuatro
y entraremos dos.

De lejanas tierras
venimos a verte.
Nos sirvió di guía
la Estrella de Oriente.

Al niño lo llevan
con mucho cuidado,
porque el rey Herodes
quiere degollarlo.

9. Carol

Come, little shepherds,
we're going to Bethlehem,
where the Child has been born,
the child Emmanuel.

Chorus
The Christmas gift,
we ask of you, lady!
For four of us have come
but only two will enter.

From far off lands
we come to see you.
The Eastern Star
served as our guide.

The child is borne
with loving care
because Herod the King
desires to slay him.

About the Songs

"Vuela, suspiro," a nineteenth century folk song, uses the habañera dance rhythm of Cuba. The song is popular throughout Latin America.

"¿Donde vas, Alfonso Doce?" comes from Spain and refers to Alfonso XII (1857-1885), the popular ruler of Spain from 1874-1885.

"A cantar a una niña" is also popular throughout Latin America. Here it is arranged as a lullaby.

"Mi mamá me aconsejaba" is a well-known folk song in Mexico. The text tells of a mother cautioning her son about the attractions of young love.

"Nesta rua" is a very popular folk song in Brazil. Its haunting melody and evocative text create one of the most beautiful Latin American folk songs.

"Una tarde fesquita de Mayo" is a more recent Latin American folk song, probably originating near the end of the nineteenth century.

"El Capotín" is actually two songs that have long been sung together: "No me mates" and "El Capotín."

"Al pasar por Sevilla" is a Spanish folk song well-known in Latin America.

"Villancico" is a Spanish Christmas carol but the text comes from Puerto Rico.

About the Writers

Bruce Trinkley, Professor of Music at The Pennsylvania State University, teaches composition, orchestration, and opera literature, and conducts the Penn State Glee Club. He received his undergraduate and graduate degrees in composition from Columbia University, where he studied with Otto Luening and Jack Beeson and conducted the Columbia University Glee Club. Winner of the BMI National Varsity Show Award for the best original student musical in the United States, Trinkley went on in 1976 to write the music for the Pennsylvania Bicentennial Wagon Train Show, which played more than 2000 performances throughout the country. The composer of incidental music, songs and choruses for over twenty theatre and dance productions, Trinkley has also written extensively for choral ensembles. His theatre works include six operas, a ballad opera, two operettas, two musical comedies, and several dramatic cantatas. Recent works include *Santa Rosalia*, a cantata inspired by paintings of the Colombian artist, Fernando Botero, which was filmed for PBS presentation; *Cold Mountain* for piano trio, based on poems by the Tang Dynasty poet Han-shan, commissioned for the Castalia Trio's concert tour to China; and *One Life: The Rachel Carson Project*, a cantata for women's voices about the life and works of the founder of the environmental movement. His most recent work, a children's opera entitled *The Prairie Dog That Met the President*, is based on a true incident from the Lewis and Clark expedition and was premiered by the Marjorie Lawrence Opera Theatre.

J. Jason Charnesky teaches literary theory, English, and cultural studies at The Pennsylvania State University. He has collaborated with Bruce Trinkley on a number of choral and dramatic works including: *Santa Rosalia*, a cantata dedicated to all those living with AIDS; and *Ever Since Eden*, a triptych of one-act comic operas which comprises *Eve's Odds*, *Golden Apple* and *Cleo*.

Special thanks to Robert Lima, Professor Emeritus of Spanish and Comparative Literature, The Pennsylvania State University, for literal English translations, and to Richard Kennedy, Associate Professor of Voice, School of Music, The Pennsylvania State University, for pronunciation guidance.

About the Recording

Nine Latin American Folk Songs accompaniment tracks were recorded at Red Rock Recording, Saylorsburg, PA

Piano - Sally K. Albrecht

Engineer - Kent Heckman

For a complete listing of vocal solo and duet collections, visit www.alfred.com